Concert Halls of the World

by Nancy Lochner

HOUGHTON MIFFLIN   BOSTON

PHOTOGRAPHY CREDITS
Cover center © QT Luong/terragalleria; **Cover background** © Map Resources; **1** © Luis CastaÒeda/The Image ProShop; **2** © Masterfile; **3** © David Ball/Alamy; **4–5** © age fotostock/SuperStock; **5** © Roland Halbe/lpn; **6** © Luis CastaÒeda/The Image ProShop; **7** © PCL/Alamy; **8** © Corbis; **9** © VIEW Pictures Ltd/Alamy; **10** © Yoshio Tomii/ SuperStock; **11** © age fotostock/SuperStock

Printed in China

ISBN 10: 0-618-89958-8
ISBN 13: 978-0-618-89958-6

13 14 15 16 17 0940 20 19 18 17 16

4500590856

Sydney Opera House

The Sydney Opera House is located in Sydney, Australia and was built in 1973. It is one of the most famous concert halls in the world.

There are several theaters within the Sydney Opera House. The three largest are the Concert Hall (2,679 seats), the Opera Theatre (1,507 seats), and the Drama Theatre (544 seats).

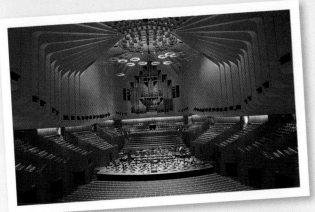

Concert Hall

You can use a place-value chart like this to compare and order the numbers of seats in these three theaters.

	thousands	hundreds	tens	ones
Concert Hall	2	6	7	9
Opera Theatre	1	5	0	7
Drama Theatre		5	4	4

Start at the left to compare the digits in the thousands column. Two thousand is greater than 1 thousand, so 2,679 is the greatest number. That tells us that the Concert Hall has the greatest number of seats.

Read·Think·Write Continue comparing digits. Which theater has the least number of seats?

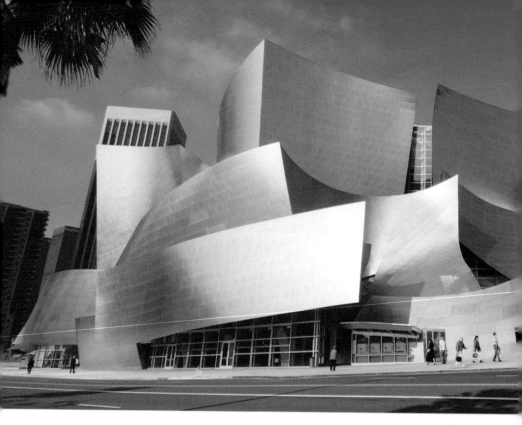

Walt Disney Concert Hall

The Walt Disney Concert Hall is in Los Angeles, California. It was completed in 2003 and was designed to look like a ship with billowing sails.

The Walt Disney Concert Hall has 2,265 seats. It is part of a larger complex called the Music Center. Other theaters in the Music Center are the Dorothy Chandler Pavilion (3,197 seats), the Ahmanson Theatre (maximum 2,000 seats), and the Mark Taper Forum (752 seats).

Interior of Walt Disney Concert Hall

Another way to order numbers is to use a number line like this one.

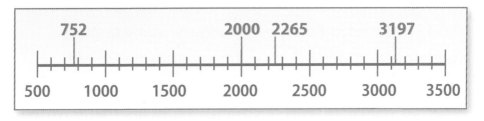

Read·Think·Write Name the theaters in order, from fewest seats to most seats.

Hungarian State Opera House

The Hungarian State Opera House opened in 1884 and is located in Budapest, Hungary. Many famous composers and conductors have performed there.

This magnificent building has red velvet seats, white marble staircases, and decorations that are made with 24-karat gold.

Originally, the Hungarian State Opera House had approximately 2,400 seats. Almost 100 years later, it was renovated to provide more room for the stage, and now it has 1,300 seats.

Read·Think·Write Did the Hungarian State Opera have more seats when it was originally built, or after it was renovated?

Interior of Hungarian State Opera House

Royal Albert Hall of Arts and Sciences

The Royal Albert Hall is located in London, England. It was opened in 1871 by Queen Victoria, and is named after her husband, Prince Albert.

The dome on top is made of painted glass and steel.

Interior of Royal Albert Hall

Over the years, the oval hall has been used for a variety of events, including classical music recitals, rock concerts, and sporting events. The Royal Albert Hall has a seating capacity of 5,222.

	thousands	hundreds	tens	ones
Royal Albert Hall	5	2	2	2
Hungarian State Opera House	1	3	0	0

Read·Think·Write Does the Royal Albert Hall have more seats or fewer seats than the Hungarian State Opera House?

Vienna State Opera

The Vienna State Opera is located in Vienna, Austria. It opened in 1869 and is one of the oldest concert halls in the world. It also has one of the largest stages in Europe.

Interior of Vienna State Opera

The original stage and much of the building were destroyed in 1945. It was rebuilt in 1955, and now has a seating and standing room capacity of 2,282.

	thousands	hundreds	tens	ones
Vienna State Opera	2	2	8	2
Royal Albert Hall	5	2	2	2
Hungarian State Opera House	1	3	0	0

Read·Think·Write Put these numbers in order from greatest to least and compare the capacities of the Hungarian State Opera House, the Royal Albert Hall, and the Vienna State Opera.

1. Which has the most seats, the Concert Hall in the Sydney Opera House or the Walt Disney Concert Hall?

2. Refer to page 5. Use a place-value chart to put the numbers of seats in order from greatest to least.

3. Which of the concert halls or theaters listed in this book has the most seats? Which has the fewest?

4. Put these three seating capacities in order, from greatest to least:

   Boston Symphony Hall (Boston) – 2,625
   Renee & Henry Segerstrom Concert Hall
   (Costa Mesa) – 2,002
   Carnegie Hall (New York) – 2,804

Activity

Categorize and Classify Find the date that each of the five concert halls listed in this book was first opened. Record these numbers from least to greatest on a number line. Which one is the newest?